CW01220659

SHROPSHIRE SCHOOLS	
010010535378	
Bertrams	07/06/2010
938	£9.99
01065017	

ANCIENT GREEK ADVENTURE

Angela Royston

Published 2010 by
A & C Black Publishers Ltd.
36 Soho Square, London, W1D 3QY

www.acblack.com

ISBN   HB   978-1-4081-2438-3
       PB   978-1-4081-2695-0

Series consultant: Gill Matthews

Text copyright © 2010 Angela Royston

The right of Angela Royston to be identified as the author of this work has been asserted by her in accordance with the Copyrights, Designs and Patents Act 1988.

A CIP catalogue for this book is available from the British Library.

All rights reserved. No part of this publication may be reproduced in any form or by any means – graphic, electronic or mechanical, including photocopying, recording, taping or information storage and retrieval systems – without the prior permission in writing of the publishers.

Every effort has been made to trace copyright holders and to obtain their permission for use of copyright material. The authors and publishers would be pleased to rectify any error or omission in future editions.

This book is produced using paper that is made from wood grown in managed, sustainable forests. It is natural, renewable and recyclable. The logging and manufacturing processes conform to the environmental regulations of the country of origin.

Produced for A & C Black by Calcium. www.calciumcreative.co.uk

Printed and bound in China by C&C Offset Printing Co.

All the internet addresses given in this book were correct at the time of going to press. The author and publishers regret any inconvenience caused if addresses have changed or sites have ceased to exist, but can accept no responsibility for any such changes.

Acknowledgements

The publishers would like to thank the following for their kind permission to reproduce their photographs:

Cover: DK Images: Liz McAulay; Shutterstock **Pages:** Corbis: Mimmo Jodice 16, Gianni Dagli Orti 21; Dreamstime: Hartemink 26t, Georgios Kollidas 29; Fotolia: Elmgrover 23; Getty Images: De Agostini Picture Library 10, Hulton Archive/Nobby Clark 17b; Shutterstock: Alexey Biryukov 17t, Sean Jolly 26b, Kletr 28b, Oliver Lenz Fotodesign 6t, Galina Mikhalishina 14, Pavel Mitrofanov 15t, Paul B. Moore 5, Timothy R. Nichols 18, Panosgeorgiou 20, Yiannis Papadimitriou 13, Kenneth V. Pilon 12t, 12c, Styve Reineck 28t, James Steidl 9t, Akoinoglou Vasilis 15b, Vlas2000 4, Valentyn Volkov 11t; Topham Picturepoint: Pete Jones 24; Wikimedia Commons: 19b, Marie-Lan Nguyen 8, 9b, 11b, 12b, 19t, 22, Bibi Saint-Pol 6b, 7, 25, 27.

Contents

Athens 4
Street Parade 6
The Feast 8
Dawn Walk 10
Before the Drama 12
Best Seat 14
A Tragic Tale 16
People-Watching 18
Time Out 20
The Writers 22
What a Laugh! 24
A Sacrifice 26
The Winner is… 28
Glossary 30
Further Information 31
Index 32

Athens

I am an Egyptian boy, and a Greek slave. I have just arrived in Athens with my master, Lysanias. We have come for the Great Dionysia **festival** – a huge festival in honour of the Greek god Dionysius.

The centre of ancient Athens was the Acropolis.

City state
The city of Athens was the main city-state of ancient Greece. A city-state is a small country ruled by its city. During the 400s BC, Athens was the most powerful and **civilized** city in the ancient world.

Our arrival

Earlier today we sailed into Piraeus, the nearest port to Athens. Lysanias took a chariot from the port to Athens, but I walked with Wolf, another of Lysanias's slaves.

There were few roads between the cities in ancient Greece, so boats were the easiest way to get from one place to another.

Enjoyment for everyone

Wolf told me that the **Athenians** don't work during the festival and many plays are performed in the theatre. The men drink a lot of wine and people go crazy and enjoy themselves. Even slaves have fun. It is the one time they can play tricks and jokes on their masters without getting into trouble!

Naming slaves

Slaves were often given new names. Lysanias called his slave Wolf because he came from a fierce northern tribe.

Street Parade

The festival began with a **procession** through the streets of Athens. Wolf and I joined the **parade**. Some men carried a huge bronze statue of the god Dionysus. Others were pulling bulls with ropes around their necks. Everyone was shouting and singing.

Dionysus holds a cup of wine in his hand.

Party god
Dionysus was the god of wine. He freed people from their normal lives by making them very happy, crazy, or drunk. He was also the god of farming and the theatre.

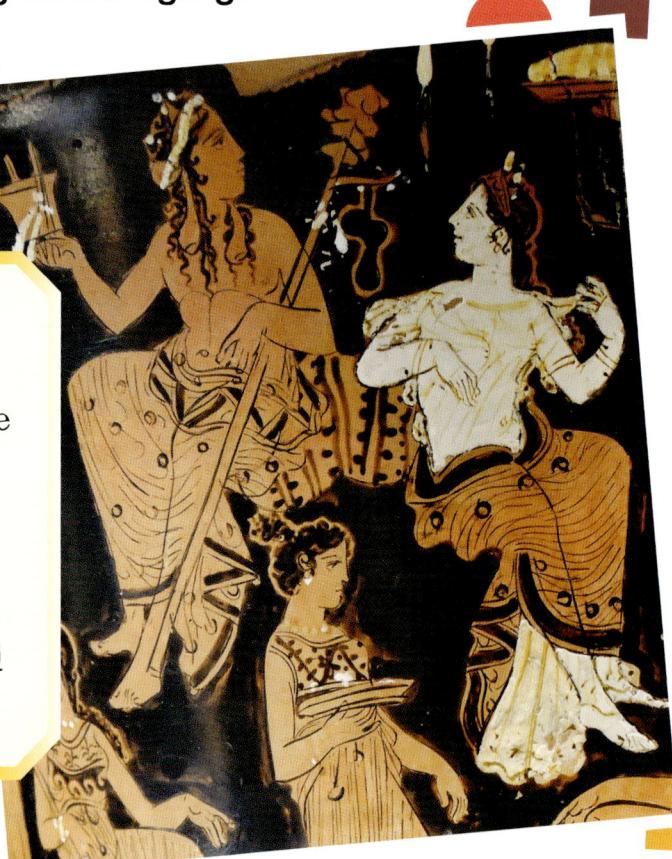

Goat men!

The men dressed as **satyrs** made me laugh. They had stuck goat's hair to their chests and backs, so they looked half goat and half man. They had also fixed goats' horns to their heads. One of them bent his head as he pranced along and butted me in the bottom!

Singing and dancing

The procession ended at the Theatre of Dionysus. Here things became more serious. Choruses of men sang songs in praise of Dionysus and danced. They competed with each other to be the best performer.

Satyrs were **mythical creatures** who were part goat and part man.

Men only

The Great Dionysia was a festival for men only. In ancient Greece, women worshipped different gods, such as the goddess Demeter, and had their own festivals for them.

The Feast

After the singing and dancing, the bulls were **sacrificed** on the altar of Dionysus. Then the meat was roasted over a fire on the altar, ready for the feast this evening.

The feast was amazing! The men lounged on couches while we slaves brought them food and wine. I carried plates of fruit and nuts, fish and olives, goat's cheese in honey, and meat. The meat smelled so good. I grabbed a piece when no one was looking and it tasted delicious! It was the first beef I had eaten since I had become a slave.

Pigs were also often sacrificed to the gods in ancient Greece.

Beef feast
A festival was one of the few times fresh meat was eaten. At the feast for Dionysus, the bones of the sacrificed bulls were burned and then presented to the god.

Dancing all night

After the food, jugglers and acrobats entertained the men. One man told such funny stories I couldn't stop laughing. Then musicians played flutes and lyres for many different dancers.

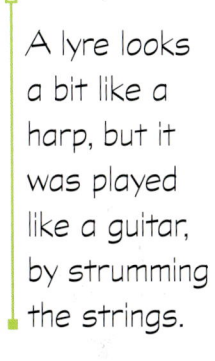

A lyre looks a bit like a harp, but it was played like a guitar, by strumming the strings.

This slave is playing an aulos, which was like a double oboe.

Time off
A festival was the only time that Greeks did not work. They did not have weekends or other holidays, so festivals were very popular.

Dawn Walk

The plays at the theatre began today. The tickets for the theatre are sold at sunrise, so I had to get up before dawn. I walked through the dark streets to the agora (marketplace). Even at this time, the agora in Athens was noisy. Some men were still making their way home from the feast, laughing and singing.

Most Greek towns had an agora. It was a place to meet and talk as well as a marketplace.

Agora

Olive

The agora

During the day the agora is the centre of the city. Shops sell food, perfume, and other things. Slaves like me were there, too, buying food and drink for the day. One shop was selling fish. Among all the sardines, there were slippery eels and octopuses. I bought cheese, lentil cakes, sardines, olives, and a large jug of wine.

A place to chat

Athenian men gather at the agora. Greek men like to talk! They discuss everything from the price of wheat to the meaning of love.

This slave is helping her mistress to put on jewellery.

A slave in every home

About half the population of ancient Greece were slaves. Almost every home had at least one slave.

How people were **enslaved**:
- taken in war (like Wolf)
- sold to pay a debt (like me)
- born to slaves

Before the Drama

At sunrise, I queued to buy our theatre tickets. Lysanias's ticket cost 2 **obols**, but I didn't have to pay for mine. Mine was paid from a special fund set up by a wealthy Athenian **citizen** for those who cannot pay – like me!

Greek obol coins.

A great man
Pericles lived from 495–429 BC and was Athens's greatest statesmen. He made Athens powerful and built many temples on the Acropolis.

A sculpture of Pericles carved in ancient Greece.

Choosing the plays

After getting the tickets, I went to the Odeon of Pericles. This building is next to the theatre and is one of the wonders of Athens. A **ceremony** was held here to decide which playwright would have his plays performed today. All the playwrights will compete to win the prize for the best play of the festival.

It's a lottery
Lots were small objects. Some lots had a special mark. The citizens and foreigners each chose one, and those that drew the special ones became the judges.

Choosing the judges

The judges of the play were chosen in a second ceremony. Several important citizens and **foreigners** drew lots to decide who would be the judges. Everyone pushed and shoved to see who had been chosen.

Lots were placed in jars, such as this one.

13

Best Seat

After the judges were chosen, I rushed to the Theatre of Dionysus to get a good seat. The wine and water sellers were already outside the theatre, so I bought a jug of spring water.

The ruins of the Theatre of Dionysus, which held about 17,000 people.

Breath-taking sight

The theatre is awesome. Rows upon rows of seats are built into the hillside so everyone can see the stage. At the very front was a row of grand, single chairs. I sat on one. It had the best view, but I was told to get off! Those seats were reserved for the priests of Dionysus, the judges, and other important people.

Choosing a seat

I climbed about halfway up the stairs and chose a seat right in the middle. I wanted to see and hear everything. Lysanias and Wolf arrived some time later. Lysanias took the food and the wine I had bought in the agora and went to sit with his friends.
Wolf sat with me.

Choosing the best

The judges watch all the plays and, at the end of the festival, they decide which playwright is the best.

Amphora jug for holding wine.

Jugs and vases

Amphoras are jugs and vases that were used to hold water, wine, olive oil, and other liquids. Many of them were decorated with pictures of Greek people doing everyday things.

A Tragic Tale

We saw three plays today, but the first one, which was a tragedy, was the best.

No women allowed! In Greek theatre there were just three male actors. They played all the different parts, including the women characters.

Plays were performed in the area in front of the seats.

The chorus

The play began when twelve people came out and formed a group at the front of the circular stage. They are called the chorus and they explained what the play was about and, as the play went on, they explained what was happening.

An ancient Greek mask.

The actors

Then three actors appeared from the skene, a wooden building at the back of the stage. They each wore brightly coloured clothes and a mask. The mask told you which of the characters the actor was playing.

Murder!

Towards the end of the play, one character was murdered. We heard him scream behind the skene, and then his "body" was wheeled on to the stage on a platform. I thought he was really dead, and cried out, but Wolf laughed at me. When the actor reappeared as another character, I realized he was still alive after all!

Sometimes, modern actors wear masks when they perform Greek plays.

Stage temple

The skene was painted to look like a temple. It had several doors through which the actors came and went.

17

People-Watching

In between the plays people talked to each other. The audience was mostly men. Respectable women were not allowed. Wolf and I discussed everyone's clothes.

Women wore long chitons down to their ankles. Men wore short chitons.

The chiton

Greek men and women all wear a chiton. This is a large rectangular piece of colourful material. It is wrapped around the body to make a kind of tunic. Then it is pinned at the shoulders and down the arms to make sleeves. You can tell who is rich or important because their chitons are fancier and have gold threads running through the material.

Woman

Man

18

Jewellery and make-up

Most of the women were colourfully dressed. They wore bracelets and ear-studs, and had ribbons in their hair. They had covered their faces with **white lead** to make themselves look pale, and had red **rouge** on their cheeks. Some of them even had make-up around their eyes!

Jewellery, such as this earring, was often made from gold.

Some women plaited their hair and pinned the plaits over their heads.

A woman's life

Most Athenian women stayed at home all the time. They only went out to go to:

- a woman's festival
- a funeral
- visit a woman neighbour

Ancient Greeks sometimes wore sandals, but they mostly went barefoot. And what did they wear under their chitons? Nothing!

Time Out

During the break between plays, people ate and drank. Wolf and I soon finished our food, but Wolf was still hungry. Lysanius says he is always hungry as a wolf!

Olive trees still grow in Greece, as they did in ancient times.

Toilet in the trees

We went look for olives to eat, but the olive grove stank! These Greeks do not mind where they wee or poo – they go in the olive grove, in the street, or wherever they are.

Public toilets

Some public buildings in ancient Greece did have toilets. They probably had wooden seats and the sewage collected in pits dug below them.

This ancient Greek statue shows a woman using a public toilet.

Playing tricks

Wolf and I laughed as we saw other slaves play tricks on their masters. They would never get away with it normally, but the festival is a time when trick-playing is allowed.

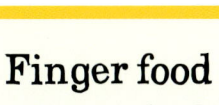

Finger food

The ancient Greeks never used a fork, but ate with their fingers instead. They put the food on flatbread or in a bowl. They used a spoon for soup and a knife to cut food.

The Writers

Lysanius had drunk too much wine and was getting angry, so I hid myself behind the skene. This was where the actors and playwrights were gathered.

Famous playwright

One man was talking with a group of people. He was Sophocles, the most famous playwright and philosopher ever. And he was just an arm's length away from me!

Sophocles lived from 495–406 BC. He wrote tragedies.

Furious playwright!

Another man was shouting and waving his arms. Someone told me that the angry man was Euripides, a famous playwright. He was furious because Aristophanes had written a play that made fun of him.

Happy or sad?
Aristophanes's play was a comedy. This meant that it was light-hearted and had a happy ending. Tragedies are plays about human suffering.

Actors wore masks that showed a laughing face to perform a comedy. A mask with a sad face was worn for a tragedy.

Played today
Plays written by Sophocles, Euripides, and Aristophanes are still performed today. Although all the actors in ancient Greece were men, many of the plays were about strong and powerful women.

What a Laugh!

Today I saw the funniest play. It was a comedy by Aristophanes, the playwright who made Euripides so angry, and was called *Birds*.

Sky city

Two old men, who were fed up with living in Athens, got the birds to agree to build a city in the sky — between the gods and Earth. The two actors then changed into birds. They wore long, colourful robes with lots of feathers stuck to them. A wooden crane lifted them into the air so that they swooped and flew like birds.

A modern production of *Birds*.

Birds rule!

The new city in the sky had very different laws from Athens. This made the audience cheer and shout! Once the birds controlled the skies, they stopped all the people's sacrifices reaching the gods. The gods began to starve to death. At the end, the gods made peace with the birds and everyone celebrated.

The chorus
In some plays the chorus sang, danced, and played musical instruments. In *Birds* the chorus imitated the songs of birds.

Two of the men in this chorus are playing lyres, while a third man dances.

Food fight!
The audience at a Greek play could be very noisy. If they did not like what was happening on stage, they threw things, such as food, at the actors.

A Sacrifice

This evening, Lysanias allowed me to go to the temple of Athena to make a sacrifice. Athena is the goddess of Athens but also the goddess of wisdom. I want Athena's help to pay off the debt to Lysanias, which forced my father to sell me into slavery.

The goddess Athena.

Parts of the Parthenon still stand on the Acropolis in Athens today.

Athena is shown here serving wine to the god Herakles.

The Parthenon

I climbed up the hill that is called the Acropolis and arrived at the Parthenon, the temple to Athena. There are many temples up here, but the Parthenon is the most important one. I left some food as a sacrifice to the goddess. I hope Athena will give me wisdom, and help me to make enough money to buy my freedom.

I left the temple and stood on the steps outside. I could see Athens below and beyond it the sea, the same sea that laps at the shores of my country. I hope I shall return there one day as a free man.

Fair goddess

As well as being the goddess of wisdom, Athena was the **champion** of **justice**, the goddess of household arts and crafts, and the **guardian** of Athens.

Money-making

Slaves in Athens earned some money. They could also make extra money by, for example, making wooden carvings and selling them.

The Winner is…

Today was the last day of the festival. There was another procession, but first the judges announced the winning playwrights — one for the best tragedy and one for the best comedy. Aristophanes only got second prize for his comedy, yet his play was by far the best!

The winning playwright was given a wreath of ivy.

Plays are still performed today in the ancient Greek theatre in Taormina on the Italian island of Sicily.

Back to real life

After the procession, everyone went home. Most people lived in or around Athens, and so they walked. The rest of us went to the port to board a ship. As we waited for the ship, Lysanias turned to me and said, "Now the festival is over, life returns to normal." That means working hard, doing whatever he says, and no tricks, or answering back. I hope Athena hears my prayers!

Here today
Many ancient theatres still exist in Greece and in places where the Greeks settled. They include Epidauros in Greece and Taormina in Sicily.

Demeta was the goddess of crops. Her festival celebrated the planting of new wheat crops.

Spring festival
The Great Dionysia was held in spring. In the autumn there was a three-day drama festival which only women went to. It was held in honour of the goddess Demeter at her temple at Eleusis, about 20 kilometres (about 12 miles) from Athens.

Glossary

Athenian a citizen of Athens

ceremony a special occasion on which something particular happens

champion someone who supports an idea or cause

citizen a person who belongs to a country or state and who therefore has certain rights

civilized having developed human achievements, such as art, ideas, architecture, and social customs

enslaved made a slave

festival special time in which something, such as a god, is celebrated

foreigner someone who comes from another country

guardian someone who looks after something special, such as a child or a city

justice fairness

mythical creature a living being or animal that exists only in a myth or myths

obol a coin in ancient Greece

parade a show that takes place along the streets of a town or city

procession when people put on a show along the streets of a town or city

rouge red make-up used on the cheeks or lips

sacrificed offered to the gods or a higher authority. Animals sacrificed to the gods were killed first

satyrs spirits of the countryside who were Dionysus' friends

white lead white make-up used to make the skin look pale

Further Information

Websites

BBC website about ancient Greece. Click on Athens to find out more about slavery and how Athens was governed at:
www.bbc.co.uk/schools/primaryhistory/ancient_greeks/

This website links you to other websites about ancient Greece. Click on Ancient Greece for Kids at:
www.kidskonnect.com/content/view/254/27/

This British Museum website takes you on a tour of a model of the Theatre of Dionysus in ancient Athens. Find out all about the theatre in ancient Greece at:
www.ancientgreece.co.uk/festivals/explore/exp_set.html

Books

Ancient Greeks (Creative History Activity Pack) by Jane Bower. David Fulton (2003).

Explore History Ancient Greece by Jane Shuter. Heinemann (2005).

Ancient Greece by Andrew Solway and Peter Connolly. Oxford University Press (2001).

I Wonder Why Greeks Built Temples by Fiona MacDonald. Kingfisher (2002).

Index

Acropolis 4
agora 10–11
amphoras 15
Aristophanes 23, 24–25
Athena 26, 27

bulls 6, 8

chitons 18, 19
chorus 16, 25
city-state 4
clothes 18, 19
comedy 23, 24–25, 28

dancing 7, 9, 25
Dionysius 4, 6, 7, 8

Euripides 23

festival 4–9
food 8, 11, 21, 25, 27

goddesses 26, 27, 29
gods 4, 6, 7, 8, 9

jewellery 11, 19
judges 13, 15, 28

make-up 19
marketplace 10–11
masks 17, 23
music 9, 25

parade 6
Parthenon 26–27
Pericles 12
plays 13, 15, 16–17, 22–25, 28
playwrights 22–23, 28
procession 6, 28, 29

sacrifice 8, 25, 26–27
satyrs 6
skene 17, 22
slaves 4, 5, 11, 21
Sophocles 22
statue 6

temple 17, 26–27
theatre 6, 7, 10, 11–25, 28
tragedy 16–17, 28